NAILED IT!

Extreme
BASE
JUMPING

Virginia Loh-Hagan

⊖ 45th Parallel Press

Published in the United States of America by Cherry Lake Publishing
Ann Arbor, Michigan
www.cherrylakepublishing.com

Content Adviser: Liv Williams, Editor, www.iLivExtreme.com
Reading Adviser: Marla Conn, ReadAbility, Inc.
Photo Credits: ©Hazan/Shutterstock.com, cover, 1; ©Alexander Cher/Shutterstock.com, 5; ©Galyna Andrushko/Shutterstock.com, 6; ©Christophe Michot/Shutterstock.com, 9; ©Elimantas Buzas/Shutterstock.com, 10; ©agap/Shutterstock.com, 12; ©Imagemaker/Shutterstock.com, 15; ©Viceandvirtue/Dreamstime.com, 17; ©Hdsidesign/Dreamstime.com, 19; ©Adventure_Photo/istockphoto.com, 20; ©Imagemaker/Shutterstock.com, 23; ©edg/Shutterstock.com, 25; ©Alfredo Martinez/Red Bull Content Pool/Alamy, 26; ©Jacomstephens/istockphoto.com, 28; ©Trusjom/Shutterstock.com, multiple interior pages; ©Kues/Shutterstock.com, multiple interior pages

45th Parallel Press is an imprint of Cherry Lake Publishing.

Library of Congress Cataloging-in-Publication Data

Loh-Hagan, Virginia.
  Extreme BASE jumping / Virginia Loh-Hagan.
     pages cm. -- (Nailed It!)
  Includes bibliographical references and index.
  ISBN 978-1-63470-022-1 (hardcover) -- ISBN 978-1-63470-076-4 (pdf) -- ISBN 978-1-63470-049-8 (paperback) -- ISBN 978-1-63470-103-7 (ebook)
  1. BASE jumping--Juvenile literature. 2. Extreme sports--Juvenile literature. 3. ESPN X-Games--Juvenile literature. I. Title.

GV770.26.L65 2015
797.5--dc23

2015006290

ABOUT THE AUTHOR

Dr. Virginia Loh-Hagan is an author, university professor, former classroom teacher, and curriculum designer. In college, she jumped off a bunk bed and broke her toe. No more jumping for her. She lives in San Diego with her very tall husband and very naughty dogs. To learn more about her, visit www.virginialoh.com.

Table of Contents

Anything Is Possible!

What did J. P. de Kam do? What did Jarret Martin do?
How did they do the impossible?

J. P. de Kam is on a 2,300-foot-tall (700 meters) cliff. A cliff is a high, steep mountain edge. He is in Lauterbrunnen Valley. It's in Switzerland. More than 30 BASE jumpers have died in this valley.

De Kam isn't scared. He's wearing a fuzzy animal suit. He fills his mouth with "dragon fuel." Fuel is a liquid that starts fires. He grabs a **torch**. He jumps off the cliff. Then blows the fuel at the torch. He blows flames! He drops down. The fire trail follows him. He does a spin. Then he pulls his canopy. A **canopy** is a special **parachute**. It's like an umbrella. It slows him down as he lands.

De Kam is a professional fire-breather. He's also an experienced BASE jumper. He combined these two loves. He made the first fire-breathing BASE jump.

Jarrett Martin had an accident. He was 18 years old. He had already completed 2,800 BASE jumps. He wanted to try

Lauterbrunnen Valley attracts extreme sports fans. It's one of the few places that allows BASE jumping.

Jarrett Martin jumped in the Norwegian fjords. Fjords are narrow bodies of water between steep cliffs.

something new. He combined **paragliding** and BASE jumping. He jumped from a cliff. His canopy didn't work. He fell. He broke his back. He hurt his organs. He was **paralyzed**. He couldn't move his legs. He lost all feeling from his chest down.

He got better. He asked, "When can I start skydiving again?"

Six months later, he was BASE jumping. He didn't quit. He said, "Anything is possible." Martin did 11 BASE jumps in four days. He started 3,000 feet (914 m) above ground. He jumped in his wheelchair. He's the first person with a disability to do such a jump.

Spotlight Biography: Nasser Al Neyadi

In 2010, Nasser Al Neyadi jumped off the world's tallest building. It's called Burj Khalifa. It's 2,716 feet (828 m) high. It's almost as tall as two Empire State Buildings. It's in the city of Dubai. Dubai is in the United Arab Emirates. Al Neyadi free-fell at nearly 100 miles (161 kilometers) per hour. His canopy launched. He floated to a safe landing. He has also jumped from Mount Everest. It's the tallest mountain in the world. It's called the "Roof of the World." Al Neyadi said, "When I am in a bad mood or not feeling good, I go for a jump. I come back feeling fresh, feeling great again."

More Than Skydiving!

What does BASE jumping mean? How are skydiving and BASE jumping alike and different? What is a canopy? What is a wingsuit? How did BASE jumping develop?

BASE jumpers are similar to skydivers. They both jump from high places. But only skydivers jump from airplanes. BASE jumpers jump from fixed objects. That means the objects don't move.

BASE stands for those objects: Buildings, **antennas**, **spans**, and earth. Antennas are towers. Spans are bridges. "Earth" means jumping from structures in nature.

BASE jumpers jump from lower heights than skydivers.

This doesn't make it safer. BASE jumping is more dangerous. Skydivers have more time to open a parachute. BASE jumpers only have a few seconds. Skydivers have sky around them. BASE jumpers risk hitting objects.

BASE jumpers use their body. They control where they are going. They enjoy the **free fall**. They do this for as long as possible. They pull the canopy to start landing.

A BASE jumper wears a harness. It wraps around the body. It holds a backpack. The canopy is in the backpack.

Winds blow around objects such as cliffs and buildings. These winds affect the canopy.

The canopy is different from skydiving parachutes. It looks like a bird's wing. Skydiving parachutes can look like a balloon top. A canopy is like a rectangle. It has handles. Jumpers use the handles to steer. This means BASE jumpers don't fall. They glide, or fly.

BASE jumpers don't have backup parachutes like skydivers. They pack their canopies carefully. There can be no mistakes.

Extreme BASE Jumping: Know the Lingo

Aerial: tricks in the air

Chute: short for parachute

CRW: canopy relative work—moving two or more canopies close together while falling

Dead air exit: jumping from a fixed object, all BASE jumps start in dead air

FJC: first jump course

Flare: turn

Heading: reference point on the ground

Launch: the actual jump

PLF: parachute landing fall

Rig: equipment or gear

Running exit: running into the jump

Stack: a formation where canopies are stacked one on top of the other

Track: flying in a forward direction

Michael Pelkey and Brian Schubert jumped off El Capitan. It's in Yosemite National Park.

Some BASE jumpers wear **wingsuits**. Wingsuits are designed to catch air. They help jumpers fly. There's webbing between the legs and under the arms.

The first BASE jump was in 1783. Louis-Sebastien Lenormand jumped from a tower. He was in France. He was testing his parachute.

BASE jumping developed from skydiving. Bored skydivers wanted new thrills. Jumping from airplanes wasn't enough.

The first modern BASE jump was in 1966. Michael Pelkey and Brian Schubert jumped off a cliff. It was 3,000 feet high.

Carl Boenish is the "father of BASE jumping." He created the word BASE. He published the first BASE jumping magazine. He helped develop the sport.

"The first modern BASE jump was in 1966."

Jumping from Buildings and Antennas

What does it mean to jump off buildings? What does it mean to jump off antennas? What are some examples?

BASE jumpers jump off buildings. Buildings need to be at least 50 stories high. This gives jumpers enough time to free fall. Then they open their canopies. Most jumpers jump outside buildings. But Russell Powell jumped from inside St. Paul's Cathedral. It's in London. It's 225 feet (68.6 meters) tall.

Jeb Corliss wanted to jump off the Empire State Building. He tried to sneak in. He was caught. He was **banned**. He was not allowed to go there again. He's known as "The

Birdman." He's always dreamed of flying. When he was 6 years old, he watched birds fly. He told his aunt, "When I get older, I'm going to do that." His aunt said humans couldn't fly. Jeb said, "Maybe you can't. But I'm going to."

BASE jumpers jump off tall TV and radio antennas. They must have permission from the owners. They have to be careful. They could get electric shocks.

BASE jumping from buildings in cities is dangerous.

The Eiffel Tower in Paris is an antenna. It is 1,063 feet (324 m) tall. Hervé le Gallou jumped the Eiffel Tower 40 times. He escaped the cameras and guards. Gary Connery jumped through the center of the Eiffel Tower. The weather was terrible. The wind pushed him to the side. He hit the road.

NAILED IT!

When Extreme Is Too Extreme!

Stanislav Aksenov has two passions. He enjoys BASE jumping and body piercing. He does not use a regular harness or straps. He hooks the canopy into the body piercings on his back. His skin holds up his body. His skin stretches under his weight. He did this stunt at 1,300 feet (396 m) above the ground. He jumped from high cliffs. He was in the Lauterbrunnen Valley. He dangled from the flesh of his own back. He did this for more than two minutes. He landed safely in a field.

It is illegal to jump from the Eiffel Tower.

He just missed traffic. He broke ribs. He spent a week in the hospital.

The Willis Tower is 1,730 feet tall (527 m). The Red Bull Air Force team made the first BASE jump from this tower. They did it for a movie. The movie is *Transformers: Dark of the Moon.* They flew between buildings. They wore wingsuits. They've done more than 6,000 BASE jumps.

Jumping from Spans and Earth

What does it mean to jump off spans? What does it mean to jump off the earth? What are some examples?

BASE jumpers jump from spans. Spans are natural or man-made objects. They go across a valley or water. They include bridges and arches.

Dan Schilling was in the military. He jumped out of military planes. He wanted a new challenge. BASE jumping is his hobby.

Schilling jumped off the Perrine Bridge 201 times in 24 hours. He had to jump about every six minutes. A **crane** lifted him to the top. A crane is like a machine arm.

He messed up a couple of times. Other people packed his canopy. One time it didn't work. He crashed into the side of the river. There was another accident. His steering broke. He still landed in the water. He didn't quit.

BASE jumpers jump from earth. They look for high places. They jump from cliffs and mountains.

The Fisher Towers are mountains in Utah. They look like towers. They are spiky. They are packed closely together. There are lots of dangerous winds.

Jumpers can jump from Idaho's Perrine Bridge. It is 486 feet (148 m) above the Snake River.

Jumpers combine BASE jumping with mountain climbing. They have to get to the top somehow!

Miles Daisher, Andy Lewis, and J. T. Holmes jumped off the Fisher Towers. They jumped from a **mesa** to the top of

Getting Your Body Ready!

Heather Swan and her husband, Glenn Singleman, climbed Mount Meru. It's in Africa. They climbed for 22 days. They reached 21,667 feet (6,604 m). They put on wingsuits. They jumped off the cliff. They were in free fall for over two minutes. They opened their canopies. They glided to a glacier. They broke the record for highest BASE jump. They had to prepare for this. They practiced 150 skydives. They wore wingsuits for 60 of those. They practiced hiking the mountain. They took pictures. They studied wind patterns. Glenn said, "Once you know the real risks and prepare yourself against them, then you know the real reward. In our case, it was being able to fly off one of the most beautiful mountains in the world."

a tower. A mesa is high but has a flat top. They jumped in wingsuits.

BASE jumpers like to do tricks. Espen Fadnes jumped off a cliff in Norway. He spread his wingsuit. At the same time, Bjorn Magne Bryn skydived from a helicopter. They met mid-air. They joined together. Fadnes acted like a magic carpet. Bryn "surfed" on top of him. Fadnes shouted, "We're flying!" Then he broke away. A BASE jumper and a skydiver connected in mid-air. This had never been done before.

Fadnes likes flying. He said, "I do small movements with my shoulders and arms to control the way I move through the air. It tricks me into thinking I am turning into a bird for a short period. I know I am not, but that is how it feels. It is such a strange feeling doing something so inhuman."

"Fadnes shouted, 'We're flying!'"

BASE jumpers refuse to believe that humans can't fly.

Challenges

What are some dangers of BASE jumping? What are some challenges BASE jumpers face? How do BASE jumpers challenge themselves? How are they reinventing the sport?

BASE jumping is dangerous. People have died. Jumpers get trapped in their canopies. Canopies don't open. Or they open too late. Jumpers get hooked onto objects. They slam into objects. Jumpers drown after landing in water.

In many places, BASE jumping is illegal. Illegal means it is not allowed by law.

BASE jumpers fight for places to jump. Some BASE jumpers have picked locks. They have climbed fences.

They have tricked security guards. Some break laws.

The first BASE jumpers had to sneak into places. Police didn't want them to hurt themselves or others. BASE jumpers could go to jail.

No Limits is an extreme sports team. Once they dressed up like priests. They hid their canopies under their robes. They tricked security. They jumped off the Palace of Culture. It's 778 feet (237 m) tall. It's in Poland. They landed safely. They sped off in a car. They got away.

BASE jumping is not allowed in cities. It's dangerous for BASE jumpers. It's also dangerous for people on the ground.

Miles Daisher is a member of the Red Bull Air Force. He pushes the limits of BASE jumping and skydiving.

Miles Daisher is extreme. He jumped from the inside of a hotel. He jumped from the top floor. It has 19 stories. He climbed up 29,000 feet (8,839 m) to do so. He parachuted down the center. He did this 57 times in one day.

BASE jumpers invent new ways to have fun. Daisher created "skyaking." It's skydiving while sitting in a kayak. A kayak is a small boat. He does tricks in the air. He lands in water.

Dean Potter combined rock climbing and BASE jumping. He climbed rock walls. He didn't use any ropes. He only brought a canopy. If he didn't make it up, he glided down. He called this "free BASE" jumping. He was only person who did it. It's too dangerous. He didn't have much time to open his canopy. Potter died BASE jumping in 2015.

A challenge for BASE jumpers is to jump from all four

"BASE jumpers invent new ways to have fun."

BASE jumpers challenge themselves.

objects. BASE jumpers get a special number. Phil Smith did it. He was the first person. So, he is BASE 1. Carl Boenish created this system. He was the fourth person to do it. He is BASE 4.

BASE jumpers are always challenging themselves. They have to be daring. They have to be smart. They have to take chances. They have to jump.

Voice from the Field: Dean Potter and Whisper

Dean Potter had a miniature Australian cattle dog. Her name is Whisper. Whisper is the world's first wingsuit-wearing BASE-jumping dog. She jumped from a 13,000-foot (3,962 m) mountain. They were in the Swiss Alps. Potter created a special backpack to safely hold Whisper on his back. He did test runs with a stuffed animal. He made sure Whisper was okay with speed. He rode around with her on his bicycle and motorcycle. He drove about 80 miles (129 km) an hour. Whisper even had her own goggles, or doggles. Potter said, "Something almost made me crumble when I started putting the dog on my back. Nothing is going to happen to her. I'm ready. I'm not going to blow this flight." Watch Potter talk about Whisper's BASE-jumping adventure: http://video.nationalgeographic.com/video/short-film-showcase/dog-base-jump.

Did You Know?

- BASE jumping was almost called BEST jumping. BEST stands for "bridge, earth, span, tower."

- Before jumping, BASE jumpers drop a weighted ribbon to test the wind. They watch how the wind makes the ribbon move. If the wind blows toward them, it might push them into an object.

- An Australian man jumped from the Statue of Liberty. He noticed an open door. It led to the torch. He was arrested afterward. He said, "I just couldn't help myself."

- Espen Fadnes tried to jump off the tallest building in Bangkok. He misjudged the landing. He crashed into a billboard. He fell onto the street below. He cut his left foot. He said the crash was "more embarrassing than painful."

- The idea of humans flying is not new. Chinese people jumped from cliffs in the 1100s. They used homemade parachutes. Leonardo da Vinci drew parachutes that used a wooden frame.

- John van Horne jumped from a tower. It's in Malaysia. It's 1,381 feet (421 m) high. He landed in a swimming pool. He landed in the middle of a pool party! It was on the roof of another tall building.

Consider This!

TAKE A POSITION! Many places ban BASE jumping. Professional BASE jumpers are experienced jumpers. They have a lot of skills. They also use proper safety gear. Do you think they should be banned from places? Argue your point with reasons and evidence.

SAY WHAT? Skydiving and BASE jumping have similarities and differences. Learn more about skydiving. Explain how these two sports are similar. Explain how they are different.

THINK ABOUT IT! Some professional BASE jumpers don't like people sneaking into places illegally. Luke Aikins is a member of the Red Bull Air Force. He has mixed feelings about the issue. He said, "One side of me is like, 'Oh cool,' and the other side is, 'Man, it's just going to make it harder for those of us trying to do it legally in the future.'" What do you think about this issue?

SEE A DIFFERENT SIDE! Imagine you are walking in a busy city. You look up. You see a BASE jumper flying at you. How would you feel about BASE jumping from this perspective? What safety concerns would you have?

Learn More: Resources

PRIMARY SOURCES

Sky High: The True Story of a Paraplegic Skydiver, a documentary about Jarrett Martin (directed by Macaela VanderMost, 2012), http://skyhighthe-movie.com

The Man Who Can Fly, a documentary about Dean Potter (National Geographic, 2012).

McConkey, a documentary about Shane McConkey (2013), http://mcconkeymovie.com

SECONDARY SOURCES

Cohn, Jessica. *BASE Jumping.* New York: Gareth Stevens Publishing, 2013.

Hamilton, Sue. *BASE Jumping.* Edina, MN: ABDO Publishing, 2010.

Kelley, K. C. *BASE Jumping.* Mankato, MN: Child's World, 2012.

WEB SITES

ProBASE World Cup: http://probaseworldcup.com

Red Bull Air Force: http://redbullairforce.com

Glossary

antennas (an-TEN-uhz) towers used to broadcast TV, radio, cell phone, or other signals

banned (band) officially not allowed

canopy (KAN-uh-pee) a special parachute for BASE jumpers that looks like a bird's wing

crane (KRANE) a machine that looks like an arm and lifts things

free fall (FREE FAWL) flying in the air for a while after jumping and before landing

mesa (MAY-suh) a land formation that is raised with a flat top and looks like a table

parachute (PA-ruh-shoot) a piece of strong, light fabric attached to thin ropes that helps skydivers slow down their fall through the air

paragliding (pa-ruh-GLYE-ding) to soar from a cliff using a parachute that is like steerable wings

paralyzed (PA-ruh-lized) unable to move body parts, having no feeling

spans (SPANZ) man-made or natural bridges or arches that cover an opening

torch (TORCH) a wooden stick that can be set on fire and carried in one hand

wingsuits (WING-soots) one-piece outfits, with webbing between arms or legs, that help BASE jumpers fly

Index